Encyclopedia
of Birds
for Young Readers

Albatros

CONTENTS

✳ **NOT ALL OF US FLY** 4

✳ **HAVE WINGS, WILL FLY** 6

Relatives of the chicken 8

We climb trees 10

Aerobats 12

The crane and its relatives 14

Owls 16

Pigeons and doves 18

Gulls etc. 20

Ducks, geese, and swans 22

Kingfishers 24

Penguins 26

✳ **WE LIVE BY THE WATERSIDE I** 28

We live by the waterside II 30

✳ **PARROTS I** 32

Parrots II 34

✳ **SONGBIRDS I** 36

Songbirds II 38

Songbirds III 40

We're singers too 42

✳ **BIRDS OF PREY I** 44

Birds of prey II 46

Not all of us fly

No wings to speak of.

We're outstanding runners.

We make our nests on the ground.

Dad sits on the eggs till they hatch.

Birds evolved from their distant ancestors: a small group of feathered dinosaurs. Over millions of years, birds succeeded in adapting to life in a great variety of environments. Dense feathers protect them from the frosts of the Arctic and the scorching heat of the desert. Some birds spend days on end in the air, while others are at home in the water. Not all birds use the advantages given by wings and flight in the same way. A small group of runners needs no wings at all, as these birds spend their whole lives on the ground. Well-known birds that move around only on their legs include ostriches and kiwis.

Moa

This wingless giant—it was as tall as a bus—lived on the isolated islands of New Zealand several centuries ago. Humankind is responsible for its extinction.

Variegated tinamou

The only bird on this page that could apply for a pilot's license is the tinamou. It flies short distances only, however, preferring to run on the ground whenever possible.

Common ostrich

The sight of the ostrich's strong thighs tells us that it is an exceptional sprinter. It can reach speeds of up to 70 miles an hour. It lays eggs of record-breaking size too.

Variegated tinamou

Common ostrich

Southern cassowary

Emu

Greater rhea

Moa

5

Greater rhea

Greater rheas find their food on the grassy plains of South America. Often, they group together in small flocks.

Southern cassowary

Cassowaries defend themselves with dagger-sharp claws. A kick from a jumping cassowary can cause fatal injury to a human.

Emu

The emu is Australia's largest bird. It may not grow to be as large and speedy as the ostrich, but in a race it would beat the world's best athletes over distances both short and long.

Have wings, will fly

The bird kingdom is extremely colorful and varied. A bird's body, wings, beak, and legs are adapted to the way of life of its species. The body of a flighted bird commonly has light, hollow bones and air sacs to enhance breathing and enable movement, even at high altitudes, where oxygen is scarce. As aerobatics and navigation require rapid processing of large amounts of data, the brains of most birds are relatively large and powerful. The broad wingspan of the wandering albatross and the Andean condor, for instance, enables them to sail on an air current without much effort.

Wandering albatross

Thanks to its wingspan of over 10 feet, the albatross can cover hundreds of miles in a single day. It sails on air currents over the sea.

Barn swallow

The mud nests of swallows are often found on houses and farm buildings. Swallows feed on insects, which they deftly catch when in flight.

American flamingo

The beak of the elegant flamingo is well adapted for collecting and filtering out small organisms in the water. Flamingos gather in large flocks for feeding and migration.

Red-and-green macaw

Wandering albatross

Barn swallow

American flamingo

Great crested grebe

Eurasian hoopoe

Great crested grebe

The grebe is among those birds adapted for life on water. It gets its food by diving for it, and its nest is like a floating island.

Eurasian hoopoe

We find this beauty with its distinctive wing patterning and striking crest in Europe, Asia, and Africa. It uses its long beak to gather insects from the grass.

Red-and-green macaw

The feathers of the many species of parrot have a bright and varied palette. The hefty, long-tailed red-and-green macaw inhabits the tropical rainforests of South America.

Relatives of the chicken

We can see how Galliformes live by watching ordinary domestic chickens. They forage for food on the ground using their strong legs. They fly only short distances, usually away from danger.

Helmeted guineafowl

Red junglefowl

Wild turkey

Willow grouse

✳ Helmeted guineafowl

As with all birds that forage for food on the ground, the stout body of the helmeted guineafowl is not made for long flights. The Ancient Egyptians kept domesticated guineafowl in their yards.

✳ Willow grouse

The hardy willow grouse lives in cold regions of the northern hemisphere, making its nest on the ground. In anticipation of the snows of winter, it dresses in snow-white plumage.

✳ Wild turkey

The turkey cock looks impressive, particularly when it preens and spreads its tail feathers. Although it weighs over 20 pounds, it flies to the treetops with ease.

Red junglefowl

The red junglefowl, a primary ancestor of the domestic chicken, lives in the wild. The male boasts long, colorful feathers and a striking red crest on his head.

Indian peafowl

The original home of this elegant, long-trained bird is India. When courting, the male spreads out his beautiful tail feathers for the admiration of others.

Western capercaillie

This increasingly rare inhabitant of coniferous forests in Northern Europe and Russia has a diet of berries and pine needles. In the mating season the hen makes a characteristic creaking sound.

Golden pheasant

Western capercaillie

Grey partridge

Common pheasant

Indian peafowl

Grey partridge

The inconspicuous partridge lives in small groups on patches of land and in fields, where it forages for grain. In their first weeks, partridge young feed mainly on insects.

Common pheasant

Although the original home of the pheasant is Asia, humans have established pheasant communities all over the world, as it is a popular game animal. It spends its days in the fields and its nights roosting in the trees.

Golden pheasant

This species of pheasant comes from China. Thanks to its vivid colors, golden crest, and striped neck, it is often kept in an aviary—a large enclosure for housing birds—as a creature of beauty.

We climb trees

✳ Black woodpecker

In its search for insects in the wood and under the bark of trees, the woodpecker uses its strong beak as a chisel. It is such a skilled carpenter that it digs out a cavity in the trunk to make its nest in.

✳ Great spotted woodpecker

We hear the drumming of the great spotted woodpecker in the forests of Europe and Asia. When climbing tree trunks, they use their firm tail feathers for support.

✳ European green woodpecker

The European green woodpecker, too, is on the team of deft climbers. It often forages for food on the ground, and we see it in gardens and parks.

Toco toucan

The beaks of toucans and aracaris grow to a remarkable size. Yet these beaks are so light, they are no impediment to the birds' deft flight from treetop to treetop.

Chestnut-eared aracari

The diet of the chestnut-eared aracari consists mainly of the fruit of tropical trees. It is found in the forest lowlands of Amazonia and in the Andes Mountains.

Emerald toucanet

The emerald toucanet lives in the mountain forests of South America, making its nests in the hollows of trees. In addition to fruit, its diet includes eggs and small animals.

Chestnut-eared aracari

Emerald toucanet

Eurasian wryneck

Red-and-yellow barbet

Bearded barbet

Eurasian wryneck

The wryneck enjoys eating ants. Like its larger woodpecker relatives, it gathers its prey with its long, sticky tongue.

Red-and-yellow barbet

This highly visible inhabitant of the open forest plantations of Africa likes to nest in burrows in riverbanks or termite mounds.

Bearded barbet

The striking beak of the bearded barbet has tooth-like protrusions that help it gather fruit. It is found in Africa, where there is an abundance of fig trees.

Aerobats

I have weak legs but agile wings.

Common swift

Rufous-crested coquette

Sword-billed hummingbird

Marvelous spatuletail

12

✺ Rufous-crested coquette

This hummingbird with a striking red crest on its head prefers to live in the lowlands, although in the Andes Mountains in South America it can be found at altitudes over a mile above sea level.

✺ Sword-billed hummingbird

Thanks to its long beak, a hummingbird can reach into deep tubular flowers. The extraordinarily long sword-shaped beak of this species can reach places even other hummingbirds can't.

✺ Marvelous spatuletail

This rare hummingbird boasts an unusual decoration: the striking violet-blue discs at the ends of its two long tail feathers.

Common swift

When not raising its brood, the common swift spends most of its time in the air, not even coming to the ground to drink or sleep. It manages everything in flight.

Swallow-tailed hummingbird

It got its name from the shape of its tail, which looks like a swallow. It is found in the wild and in urban gardens in South America.

Violet sabrewing

In the tropical rainforest regions of Central America, this relatively large hummingbird collects nectar, notably from the flower of the banana tree. Sometimes it supplements its diet with small insects.

Violet sabrewing

Swallow-tailed hummingbird

Ruby-throated hummingbird

Long-tailed sylph

Bee hummingbird

13

Ruby-throated hummingbird

The movements of a hummingbird's tiny wings while in flight are so rapid as to be practically invisible to the naked eye. Even so, the ruby-throated hummingbird can fly several hundred miles without a break.

Bee hummingbird

At around two inches in length and around two grams in weight, the bee hummingbird is one of the smallest members of the bird kingdom. Its eggs are about the size of a coffee bean.

Long-tailed sylph

Male and female hummingbirds differ greatly from each other in appearance. Only the male long-tailed sylph boasts long purple tail feathers.

The crane & its relatives

When you have a long neck and short, rounded wings, flying isn't much fun. Birds that don't like racing about the skies search for their food calmly on the ground or in the water. Only certain migratory species embark on long flights. Cranes and bustards are among the largest and heaviest flighted birds.

14

Great bustard

The great bustard is one of the heaviest flighted birds. It feeds on plants and insects, sometimes adding a small rodent or frog to its diet.

Sunbittern

When under threat, the unobtrusive sunbittern spreads its wings, which have a distinctive orange-and-brown pattern that looks like big eyes.

Okinawa rail

This shy bird with red legs and beak is not easy to find. It flies rarely and inhabits only a small area of an island in Japan.

Grey-crowned crane

Thanks to its crest of golden feathers and red throat pouch, this noble bird is impossible to overlook, even in its natural environment. It is at home in Africa.

Red-crowned crane

The largest of the cranes, it grows to be five feet tall. It forages for food in wetlands. When courting, the male performs an elegant dance with jumps.

Kori bustard

This species of bustard lives in African grasslands. Its male presents an unusual spectacle in the mating season: to attract the female, he inflates his neck.

Eurasian coot

Kori bustard

Red-crowned crane

Corncrake

Western swamphen

Corncrake

This tiny rail nests in Europe and Asia, migrating to Africa for winter. It makes itself known by its characteristic "krek krek" call.

Eurasian coot

Coots spend most of their time in water, using the flaps of skin on their legs as paddles. They build their nests at the waterside, with twigs and aquatic plants.

Western swamphen

The western swamphen, too, is well adapted for life by the waterside and in swamps. Thanks to its long toes, it is very good at wading and climbing reeds.

Owls

I can hear you!

Striking, noble, and mysterious, owls have a curiously rotating head, a bewitching gaze, and an upright posture. Most of them are very well equipped for hunting at night. Owls have keen distance vision, as well as the ability to locate the source of a sound with superb accuracy. An owl is so quiet in flight that its prey might hear it, by the flapping of its wings as it sails through the air, but by then there is no escape.

Snowy owl

Barn owl

Burrowing owl

Long-eared owl

Elf owl

☀ Snowy owl

The snowy owl is adapted for life in the harsh wintry conditions of the Arctic tundra. Thanks to its white coat, it blends in with the snow. It hunts in daylight.

☀ Burrowing owl

The burrowing owl spends its life on the ground, building its nest in a burrow. It prefers to hunt in daylight. It lures its prey with fragrant bait comprised of droppings and food.

☀ Long-eared owl

When it is sitting in a tree, a long-eared owl isn't easy to spot: its feathers and markings look like bark. Its head is adorned with longer ear-shaped feathers.

Barn owl

A widely distributed owl with a characteristic heart-shaped veil around its eyes, it hunts small animals, especially rodents. It is active at dusk and nighttime.

Eurasian eagle-owl

The arrangement of feathers on the head of this large owl looks like a pair of ears. The body length of the largest members of the species is around two and half feet, their wingspan around six feet.

Great grey owl

Thanks to its extraordinarily sensitive hearing, the great grey owl can track movements of creatures deep under the snow.

Eurasian eagle-owl

Great grey owl

Pel's fishing owl

Northern hawk-owl

Elf owl

The world's smallest owl lives in warm, arid areas of North America. Its favorite abode is a hollow in the saguaro cactus.

Pel's fishing owl

This African owl doesn't need to master the art of silent flight, as other owls must: its specialty is fishing, and fish cannot hear it under water.

Northern hawk-owl

From the air or a branch, this quick, agile hunter follows the movements of rodents on the ground, waiting for the right moment to swoop and attack with its sharp claws.

Pigeons & doves

Pigeons and doves have relatively small heads on stout bodies. Thanks to their strong wing muscles, they are fast, tireless fliers. In flight, they make a characteristic clapping sound. From a single wild ancestor, humans have created over 1,000 breeds. Mail pigeons were first used to send messages in the time of Julius Caesar. Domestic pigeons that escaped from the farm and returned to the wild have adapted to life in cities.

Coo, coo.

Rock dove

Victoria crowned pigeon

Rose-crowned fruit dove

Green imperial pigeon

❋ Victoria crowned pigeon

This magnificent pigeon with its lace-like crest gathers fruit and seeds in the tropical forests of New Guinea. It is the world's largest living pigeon species.

❋ Rose-crowned fruit dove

In Indonesia and Australia we find a dove that could compete with the parrot for the title of world's most colorful bird. The male and female are similarly vivid.

❋ Green imperial pigeon

The flapping of the wings of the green imperial pigeon is sometimes heard in the tropical forests of Indonesia and other parts of Asia. Like most pigeons and doves, it is a fast flier.

✳ Rock dove

The ancestor of the domestic pigeon builds its nest in the wild on rocks and cliffs. Like all doves and pigeons, it moves its little head backward and forward when it walks.

✳ Common wood pigeon

This large pigeon lives in the woodlands of Europe in great numbers, building its nest in trees. It can also be sighted near human settlements. It feeds on plants.

✳ Nicobar pigeon

The Nicobar pigeon inhabits islands in tropical zones. It has long feathers on its neck and metallic green feathers on its body.

Common wood pigeon

Nicobar pigeon

Mourning dove

Common bronzewing

Eurasian collared dove

19

✳ Common bronzewing

The bright, shiny feathers of this Australian pigeon change color as the light changes. Its sustenance comes from seeds and water.

✳ Eurasian collared dove

Although it originated in Asia, in the 20th century it quickly spread across Europe. It is similar in size to the rock dove, but its body is slimmer and its tail longer.

✳ Mourning dove

Found in abundance in North America, this bird raises young several times a year. In the nest, mourning dove mothers, like other doves and pigeons, feed what's called pigeon's milk—regurgitated food—to their chicks.

Gulls etc.

We find many specializations among this aquatic lot. Some are master fliers, others exquisite divers. Most live along the coast or near expanses of fresh water. Gulls can hunt in flight. Waders can find goodies hidden along the seabed or riverbed.

Master fliers and master waders

Great black-backed gull

Atlantic puffin

Greater yellowlegs

Dunlin

Little auk

20

✳ Atlantic puffin

Not only do puffins look cute, but they are great swimmers too. They fish deep in the water, often returning to the surface with several fish in their beaks.

✳ Little auk

The heavy frosts of the Arctic are no problem for the little auk. It nests in large colonies and feeds on fish and small invertebrates.

✳ Greater yellowlegs

For the easy gathering of food in shallow water, long legs and a long beak are essential. This bird seeks out its prey underwater by means of its vision and the movements of its beak.

Great black-backed gull

The wingspan of the largest seagull is around five feet. It uses its strong curved beak to hunt, gather, and peel its food.

Black-headed gull

The gull with the characteristic noisy call has a striking dark-brown head. With the coming of winter, however, this ornamental coloring disappears.

Caspian tern

The Caspian tern, with its striking red beak, can be found by expanses of water and coasts in many parts of the world.

Caspian tern

Black-headed gull

American woodcock

Eurasian curlew

21

Dunlin

This relatively widespread inhabitant of the coast is easy to recognize by the large dark marking on its belly, reminiscent of a tuxedo suit.

Eurasian curlew

A beak bigger than that of other waders is a fine thing to have. It allows you to reach mollusks and crustaceans hidden deep in the sand of the seabed.

American woodcock

The brown-and-gray feathers of the American woodcock allow it to blend in with the wetland vegetation. When frightened, it remains motionless and trusts in its camouflage.

Ducks, geese & swans

Their beaks have small serrations at the edges, which make it easier to grip food and filter out small items from the water. As it contains an oily secretion, their dense plumage provides splendid protection against water. Their webbed feet make swimming easier.

Canada goose

Black swan

Mallard – male

Mallard – female

✳ Canada goose

North American by origin, this goose species was gradually introduced into Europe and New Zealand by human intervention. The largest individuals of this species are about three feet long.

✳ Black swan

Like the mute swan, this species has an elegant long neck and a powerful body, and it spends its life as part of a faithful pair. Unlike the mute swan, it comes from Australia and is black.

✳ Mallard

With many birds, the male and female are very different in appearance. The male duck (drake), for instance, is far more striking than his brown female companion.

✸ Greylag goose

This ancestor of the domestic goose lives on the shores of ponds and lakes, where there is an abundance of vegetation to feed on. When migrating, a flock of geese flies in a V formation.

✸ Mute swan

Elegant swans in pairs are a common adornment to lakes on castle grounds and rivers in towns. Their original habitat is the wetlands of Europe and Asia.

Greylag goose

Mute swan

Tufted duck

Harlequin duck

Mandarin duck

✸ Mandarin duck

Nature certainly went to town on the appearance of the mandarin drake! Mandarin ducks come from Asia and nest in woodlands near expanses of water.

✸ Tufted duck

With his gleaming black feathers with white flanks, the highly visible male looks like he is wearing a wedding suit. He has an overhanging crest too.

✸ Harlequin duck

The hardy harlequin duck can hunt out small aquatic creatures on the beds of wild mountain rivers. It spends its winters on rocky seashores.

Kingfishers

We dive headlong.

We recognize the kingfisher by its large head and beak, stout body, short tail, and little legs. Most species of kingfisher live in warm regions of Africa and Asia. Some excel as hunters of fish and as headlong divers.

Common kingfisher

Ruddy kingfisher

Stork-billed kingfisher

Yellow-billed kingfisher

Grey-headed kingfisher

❋ Stork-billed kingfisher

With its remarkably large beak, this kingfisher dares to defend its territory against large predators. It inhabits the forests of India and Southeast Asia.

❋ Ruddy kingfisher

The ruddy kingfisher adjusts its diet to suit its habitat. When near water, it favors fish. Otherwise, it makes do with frogs, lizards, and insects.

❋ Yellow-billed kingfisher

The yellow-billed kingfisher in our picture is obviously upset. We know this because its feathers are standing up. It lies in wait for small prey in the treetops.

❋ Common kingfisher

Found in Europe, the beautifully colored kingfisher resembles a flying gemstone. It lies in wait for its fish prey on a branch overlooking flowing water.

❋ Laughing kookaburra

This robust kingfisher from Australia is very popular. It lives in a tight family group. Its loud call sounds like laughter.

❋ Common paradise kingfisher

It lives in the primeval forests of New Guinea, where it hunts invertebrates on the ground. It nests in termite nests in trees.

African pygmy kingfisher

Common paradise kingfisher

Laughing kookaburra

Sacred kingfisher

❋ Grey-headed kingfisher

It lives in forests and scrublands in Africa, feeding mainly on insects. It nests in holes in steep riverbanks.

❋ Sacred kingfisher

In the past, Polynesians considered this kingfisher sacred, believing it could control the waves. It is widespread in Australia and New Zealand.

❋ African pygmy kingfisher

This tiny African kingfisher is about five inches long. It nests in holes in the riverbank or in termite nests.

Penguins

We fly underwater.

A penguin's wings aren't big enough to lift its stout body off the ground. But it is remarkably well equipped for underwater swimming. On the shore, penguins look amusingly clumsy. Underwater, however, they turn into graceful and fast swimmers.

Yellow-eyed penguin

Southern rockhopper penguin

Gentoo penguin

African penguin

Little penguin

✹ Southern rockhopper penguin

It uses its powerful claws to climb the super-steep cliffs, where it makes its nest. It jumps from rock to rock with surprising agility.

✹ African penguin

Not all penguins put up with biting cold and snow. This species chooses to nest on the beaches of Africa.

✹ Gentoo penguin

At home on the Antarctic Peninsula and on islands in the cool waters of the southern hemisphere, it lunches on krill that's comprised of small crustaceans and fish.

✳ King penguin

All species of penguin live in the southern hemisphere. The king penguin nests on islands in huge colonies. It feeds on fish and cephalopods.

✳ Emperor penguin

The largest of the penguins is not put off by the extreme cold of Antarctica. It can stay underwater for 20 minutes and dive to a depth of over 1,600 feet.

✳ Adélie penguin

This strong swimmer with a great sense of direction lives in Antarctica. When walking on ice, it sometimes makes things easier for itself by sliding on its belly.

King penguin

Magellanic penguin

Emperor penguin

Adélie penguin

27

✳ Little penguin

The smallest of the penguins raises its young in burrows on the seashores of Australia and New Zealand. On land, it ventures out only at night.

✳ Yellow-eyed penguin

On land, this very rare New Zealand species of penguin hides in dense vegetation. It is distinguished by its yellow eyes ringed with golden-yellow feathers.

✳ Magellanic penguin

This jacketed penguin with two black stripes—under its throat and on its chest—inhabits the cold shores of South America. The skin around its eyes and beak is pink.

We live by the waterside I.

Welcome to the fish buffet!

The genteel patrons of this fish buffet are appropriately equipped for a feast in a watery environment. The shapes of their beaks correspond with the way in which they hunt fish and other aquatic creatures. Most of them prefer to dine in the water, while others are happier on the dry banks. Boobies and gannets plunge into the water headfirst. Many of these birds have very long legs for wading with. The strong swimmers among them have webbed toes.

✳ Glossy ibis

It lives in many parts of the world, in areas with shallow water. With its curved beak, it fishes for small creatures on the bottom.

✳ Scarlet ibis

It gets its beautiful red coloring by consuming red crabs. It lives in the wetlands of South America.

✳ Roseate spoonbill

Spoonbills spend many hours of each day hunting for crustaceans and small fish at the bottom of an expanse of water, moving their spoon-shaped beak from side to side.

Scarlet ibis

Glossy ibis

Grey heron

Roseate spoonbill

Eurasian bittern

Black-crowned night heron

29

✳ Grey heron

The mighty heron lies in wait, motionless, ready to grab an unsuspecting fish by shooting out its long S-shaped neck like a harpoon.

✳ Eurasian bittern

In dense reeds the Eurasian bittern is practically impossible to spot, so effective is its camouflage. During the mating season, males draw attention to themselves with a booming call.

✳ Black-crowned night heron

It waits patiently on the bank or shore for its prey. It makes good use of its excellent vision by hunting at night and at daybreak. During the day, it rests in the trees.

We live by the waterside II.

If you like wading, it is good to have long toes. For agile movement on the surface of a lake or sea, it is good to have webbed feet, with toes pointing forward—as feet like this operate like oars. For the skilled fish-hunter, a throat pouch is a useful addition.

Northern gannet

Great white pelican

Great frigatebird

Flightless cormorant

Great cormorant

30

Northern gannet

It plunges into the water from a great height at speeds of up to 60 miles per hour, softening the impact by using its air sacs and by folding its wings against its body.

Great cormorant

Thanks to its abilities as an underwater swimmer, the great cormorant is a very successful fisherman. It nests in a large colony near water.

Flightless cormorant

On the Galapagos Islands, it has no natural enemies. As it finds all its food in the sea, it has no need for wings.

Great white pelican

Despite its size, the pelican is an excellent swimmer and a good flier. It catches fish underwater, by puffing out its large pouch.

Great frigatebird

An extraordinarily good flier, it catches fish from the air, sometimes stealing them from other birds. In the mating season, the male puffs out his red throat pouch.

Blue-footed booby

Rightly proud of its blue feet, this sea bird shows them off when courting. It often catches fish by diving for them headfirst from a great height.

Blue-footed booby

Shoebill

Hamerkop

Anhinga

Shoebill

Because of its comically large beak, at first sight we may imagine the shoebill to be clumsy. But this beak is sharp, too, and this bird can attack at lightning speed.

Hamerkop

It lives in Africa, where it inhabits wetlands, ponds, and other bodies of water, feeding mainly on amphibians and fish. It builds its nest—the largest in the bird kingdom—in the trees, from twigs and mud.

Anhinga

The long, slender anhinga is an excellent underwater swimmer. It catches fish by piercing them with its pointed beak. It tosses its prey into the air before swallowing it.

Parrots I.

Pretty boy!

Brightly colored parrots live in the tropics and southern hemisphere in great abundance. They are often bred in captivity, not only for their beauty but because they are highly intelligent and sociable. Some of them even learn to imitate human speech. Many species of parrot live to a great age. In its curved beak and very mobile tongue, the parrot has a universal tool—for the shelling of seeds, for instance. Its nimble toes (two facing forward, two back) are a great help with climbing and "handling."

✸ Hyacinth macaw

At three feet long, this is one of the world's largest parrots. Its population in the wild is under threat from illegal trappers and the deforestation of the Amazon rainforest.

✸ Red-winged parrot

This bird comes from Australia. Its diet includes fruit, seeds, flowers, and insects. Like most parrots, it builds its nest in tree hollows.

✸ Timneh parrot

This popular species is at home in Africa. It is such an excellent imitator of human speech that some individuals can learn hundreds of words.

Timneh parrot

Red-winged parrot

Budgerigar

Hyacinth macaw

Red-capped parrot

Eastern rosella

33

✸ Red-capped parrot

This multicolored Australian parrot lives as part of the same pair for its whole life, although it is often found in a larger flock.

✸ Budgerigar

The most commonly bred parrot comes from Australia. It gathers grass seeds in dry regions. It can live for one whole week without any water.

✸ Eastern rosella

It gathers its food on the ground and in the trees. When a large flock alights on a garden or orchard with ripening crops, it can give the farmers a real headache.

Parrots II.

What colors are you?

Many different models appear at the parrot fashion show, and some are fantastic. Although parrots come in many sizes and with many different markings, all have bright colors. While some species have a decorative crest, others are far less conspicuous and prefer to blend in with nature.

Red-and-blue lory

Coconut lorikeet

Palm cockatoo

Scarlet-chested parrot

34

🌸 Palm cockatoo

When worn by a parrot, a dark-gray coat is anything but boring. No one could fail to notice the red patches on this one's head, nor its large crest and extremely sharp beak.

🌸 Red-and-blue lory

These days, this endangered parrot species can be found only on one island in Indonesia. It spends all its time in the trees, where it makes its nest and gathers its food.

🌸 Coconut lorikeet

Flowers, pollen, and nectar are favorite items of the lorikeet's diet. Several close relatives of this species are similarly vivid and varied in color.

✸ Nestor kea

This inquisitive parrot comes from the highlands of New Zealand. Its intelligence is comparable to that of the chimpanzee. It can even use various tools.

✸ Yellow-collared lovebird

This small African parrot is popularly bred in captivity. Selectively bred mutations include blue feathers.

✸ Major Mitchell's cockatoo

Major Mitchell's cockatoo is an elegant pink creature. It emphasizes its beauty by occasionally fanning its crest.

Yellow-collared lovebird

Major Mitchell's cockatoo

Nestor kea

Pesquet's parrot

Cockatiel

✸ Scarlet-chested parrot

These friendly parrots are easy to tame. Their beautiful coloring differs from the male to the female—the latter doesn't have a red chest.

✸ Cockatiel

The cockatiel travels far and wide in search of food. It expresses emotion throught its crest, which it raises when surprised or excited.

✸ Pesquet's parrot

An unfeathered part of the face and a long beak are very practical when you eat juicy figs. The head of Pesquet's parrot looks rather like that of a vulture.

Songbirds I.

A tour of Europe

Several thousand bird species have singing abilities. Singing is a very practical way of making yourself known and thereby marking your territory. The sound is formed by a vocal organ called the syrinx, which, unlike the human vocal cords, can emit two notes at once. A songbird's legs and feet are adapted for comfortable perching on thin branches.

Common nightingale

The song of the nightingale is resonant and varied. We hear it during the day as well as at night, when the female sings. During winter, the nightingale flies from Europe down to Africa.

Common blackbird

Part of the blackbird population lives in the forest, where it originated. More blackbirds have adapted to life around humans, however, settling in gardens and parks.

Eurasian blue tit

With their spectacular coloring, blue tits are a splendid adornment to the bird feeder in winter. Their diet includes caterpillars and aphids, which they find in plants.

Common nightingale

Eurasian blue tit

Song thrush

Common blackbird

European robin

Common chaffinch

Song thrush

Like the blackbird, the thrush is a regular visitor to gardens, where it collects earthworms, gastropods, and insects. It can break the shell of a snail against a stone.

Common chaffinch

This very common European bird likes to sing from the treetops. The coloring of the male is more striking than that of the female.

European robin

In the woods, the little robin sometimes makes use of wild pigs to help it search for food in the churned-up ground.

Songbirds II.

A multicolored world orchestra

There are almost 6,500 songbird species in the world. No other order of birds is as large and diverse. Songbirds are abundant not only in forests of temperate zones; they can adapt to life in tropical rainforests and deserts too. We can tell the kind of food each bird prefers by looking at its beak. Seed gatherers, for instance, tend to have a blunt, cone-shaped beak.

Bohemian waxwing

Splendid fairywren

Orange-breasted waxbill

Gouldian finch

Silver-eared mesia

❋ Splendid fairywren

It has succeeded in adapting to life in the arid conditions of the Australian bush. It makes its domed nest by weaving together grasses, twigs, and spider webs.

❋ Silver-eared mesia

The vivid silver-eared mesia has a yellow beak and a striking white patch on its head. It lives in the forests of Southeast Asia.

❋ Orange-breasted waxbill

Widespread across a large area of sub-Saharan Africa, this small songbird feeds mainly on grass seeds. When it's not nesting, it moves around in a small flock.

Bohemian waxwing

Bohemian waxwings can be found in many parts of the northern hemisphere. Hunters of insects, they collect fruit in wintertime. They are especially fond of rowanberries.

Eurasian golden oriole

Its distinctive flute-like voice carries a long way. It weaves an ingenious hanging nest. Only the male has bright yellow plumage.

Wilson's bird of paradise

This extraordinary, exotic bird of paradise lives in Indonesia. Its unfeathered blue head gleams in the gloom of the rainforest.

Eurasian golden oriole

Wilson's bird of paradise

Northern cardinal

Green-headed tanager

Gouldian finch

Numbers of this magnificently colorful Australian songbird decreased sharply in the 20th century. One reason was illegal trapping for caged breeding.

Northern cardinal

The male is a vibrant red. He marks his territory with his loud song, fearlessly driving away unwanted guests. The northern cardinal lives in North America.

Green-headed tanager

In the dense vegetation of South America the vivid blue and green coloring of this bird is not as noticeable as you might think. In an aboriginal language, *tangara* means "dancer."

Songbirds III.

Are we in tune?

Great kiskadee

Green broadbill

Eastern kingbird

Scarlet flycatcher

Great kiskadee

The melodious voice of the great kiskadee can be heard over a wide area of South and Central America. A very skillful flier, it even hunts small animals and fish.

Eastern kingbird

It may be less than striking to look at, but this songbird is a deft, fearless warrior. Creatures that know it keep out of its way. It thinks nothing of attacking an eagle.

Green broadbill

An inhabitant of the dense forests of Southeast Asia, where it feeds mainly on figs, the vivid green broadbill blends in well with the foliage around it. It weaves its large hanging nest from grasses.

Blue manakin

These inhabitants of the forests of Southeast Brazil can supplement their song with dance. When they are together on a branch, the male dances for the female.

Blue-winged pitta

It builds its inconspicuous domed nest on the ground in the deciduous forests and mangroves of Southeast Asia. It also finds most of its food—insects and larvae—on the ground.

Andean cock-of-the-rock

This striking, rather large songbird lives in the cloud forests of the Andes Mountains. The female builds a nest on a suitable rock face, gluing the mud together with saliva.

Blue manakin

Andean cock-of-the-rock

Blue-winged pitta

Red-billed scythebill

Rufous hornero

Scarlet flycatcher

The scarlet flycatcher likes to show off its beautiful, colorful coat. It plumps up the feathers of its breast and stands up its red crest, especially when singing.

Red-billed scythebill

The red-billed scythebill can climb a tree trunk as deftly as a woodpecker. Its long, curved beak is the perfect tool for collecting insects from hard-to-reach places.

Rufous hornero

The large nest it builds out of clay is a remarkable thing: it looks like a bread oven. A pair of these birds needs several weeks to complete the work.

We're singers too

Although its cawing may not sound much like singing, the common crow is a songbird, as are other corvids. The crow, the raven, and the jay have uncommonly high intelligence, rather like the parrot. Corvids have excellent memories and can solve complex tasks. Sometimes they even use simple tools.

Rook

Eurasian jay

Carrion crow

Common raven

42

✸ Rook

We can tell a rook by its metallic black feathers, which gleam in the sun. Its large beak is unfeathered at the base and light in color. The rook has distinctive shaggy feathering around its legs. It moves around in a large flock.

✸ Carrion crow

The carrion crow is black all over, including its beak and legs. The tip of the beak is slightly curved. In flight, its tail is straight, while the rook flies with a rounded tail.

✸ Common raven

Unlike a rook's, a raven's beak has a feathered base. Highly intelligent, the raven can imitate the sounds of human speech.

✳ Eurasian jay

In the woods, everyone pricks up their ears when the jay lets out a piercing cry of alarm. It is a warning signal: danger is near. The jay likes to imitate sounds made by other creatures, such as the goat.

✳ Blue jay

The blue jay lives in the forests of North America. It has a good memory. In times of plenty, it stores food for the winter, much as a squirrel does.

✳ Eurasian magpie

This extraordinarily intelligent bird can recognize its own reflection in a mirror—a feat beyond the abilities of most animals. Outside of the nesting period, it gathers in small flocks.

Eurasian magpie

Blue jay

Common green magpie

Spotted nutcracker

Western jackdaw

43

✳ Spotted nutcracker

In the deciduous forests of Europe and Asia, it collects seeds—from pinecones, for instance. It likes to feed on hazelnuts too.

✳ Western jackdaw

The gray-black jackdaw is smaller than the crow. It nests in a hollow in a tree or a suitable shelter in an old house. When in flight, it likes to express itself through sound.

✳ Common green magpie

We find brightly colored species even among relatives of the crow and the raven. The common green magpie lives in the forests of South Asia, feeding on invertebrates, small mammals, and young birds.

Birds of prey I.

We have very sharp weapons!

Birds of prey are best equipped for the hunt. They have extremely good vision, and their forward-facing eyes allow them to estimate distance. Mostly, they catch their prey with their strong legs and feet and sharp claws. They use their curved beaks to tear meat into small pieces. Large-winged bird-of-prey species can glide through the air effortlessly, even when carrying a large catch. Shorter wings allow for greater maneuverability between trees.

Bald eagle

This North American eagle lives by the coast or an expanse of fresh water. Although it specializes in catching fish, it won't turn down a rabbit or other animal of similar size.

Griffon vulture

The circling of vultures in the sky is a sign that carrion is in the vicinity. A feature of the vulture's anatomy is an unfeathered neck, which comes in handy when removing flesh and entrails from a carcass.

Northern goshawk

When hunting among the trees of the forest, the northern goshawk relies on its dexterity. It has no trouble catching various birds, squirrels, and reptiles. It is widespread in temperate regions of the northern hemisphere.

Bald eagle

Northern goshawk

Eurasian sparrowhawk

Griffon vulture

Common buzzard

Pied harrier

45

Eurasian sparrowhawk

The Eurasian sparrowhawk is like an acrobatic fighter pilot. It perches in large trees to lie in wait for other birds, or it lunges at them in flight.

Common buzzard

In Europe, these birds of prey are so abundant that we often see them perching on telephone poles or in trees, following the movements of voles in the fields. In the woods, we hear their distinctive wails above us.

Pied harrier

It flies low over the ground, making a careful search of steppes or wetlands. It catches small mammals, frogs, and insects in the grasses and reeds.

Birds of prey II.

There are several world record holders among birds of prey. In terms of wing size, the Andean condor is without rival, while no other bird dives faster than the peregrine falcon. As rulers of the skies, birds of prey may seem cruel to us, but their role in maintaining the balance of nature is crucial. They prevent overpopulation of certain species and they clear the environment of carrion.

Harpy eagle

Palm-nut vulture

Northern crested caracara

Andean condor

❋ Harpy eagle

The harpy eagle is the king of South American rainforests. Despite its sizeable wingspan, it can catch sloths and monkeys in the branches of trees.

❋ Northern crested caracara

The color of the bare skin of its head expresses its mood; it changes with age too. The caracara feeds mostly on carrion or weak, sick animals.

❋ Palm-nut vulture

Although it is a predator, it prefers a vegetable diet to a meat one. It gobbles up crabs, fish, and other small animals only occasionally.

❋ Andean condor

The Andean condor has the largest wings of any bird. On a rising current of air, it can glide over 4 miles above sea level.

❋ Common kestrel

By fluttering its wings, it can stay in the air in one place, watching happenings on the ground with its keen vision. It is a fine hunter of voles in the field and pigeons in towns, thereby keeping down unwanted populations.

❋ Secretarybird

The secretarybird excels in a discipline unusual for birds—it is an outstanding runner. Having chased down its prey, it attacks it with sharp claws. It can even overpower a venomous snake.

Common kestrel

Eurasian hobby

Peregrine falcon

Secretarybird

Osprey

❋ Eurasian hobby

It may be small, but the Eurasian hobby is a very fast flier. It catches large insects in the air, and it will even hunt smaller birds. In winter, it moves from Europe and Asia all the way down to South Africa.

❋ Peregrine falcon

Diving headlong with its wings folded in, it can reach speeds of over 200 miles per hour. Humans like to use the peregrine for falconry.

❋ Osprey

The osprey, which is found all over the world, is a specialist at catching fish. Its outer toe is reversible, giving it a better grip on its catch. Its dense feathers are water-resistant.

Encyclopedia
of Birds
for Young Readers

Written by Tomáš Tůma
Illustrated by Tomáš Tůma

© B4U Publishing for Albatros,
an imprint of Albatros Media Group, 2022
5. května 1746/22, Prague 4, Czech Republic
Printed in China
by Dongguan Eastcolor Paper Products Co.,Ltd

www.albatrosbooks.com

ISBN: 978-80-00-06350-8

albatros